INTRODUCTION

What was family life like during the reign of Queen Victoria (1837–1901)? There were lots of different sorts of families. How people lived varied according to how rich they were, and where they lived. The life of a rich family in the countryside was very different from the life of a poor family in a town. Families were a good deal larger than they are now. This is partly because people had more children, and because the family often included other people who lived and worked in the home.

Most families, no matter how big or small, rich or poor, had a routine in which each person had their own part to play. This book looks at how some of the different members of the family contributed to family life in Victorian times.

CONTENTS

WHO WAS IN THE FAMILY?

The centre of family life was the home. Queen Victoria's husband, Albert, said "Those under our roof form our household, and so they are all part of our family." Albert was trying to explain what an ideal Victorian family was like.

The head of the house – usually a man – owned or rented the home and earned the money to run it. If the father was dead, or away from home (because he was a soldier, sailor or seaman), the mother was the head of the house.

Most married women were expected to stay at home. They had to look after the children, cook the meals and clean the house. In poorer homes, women did this work themselves. Rich women had servants to do the work, but they had to make sure it was done properly.

▷ **A doctor's family play croquet in the garden.** The servants bring out drinks for them.

▽ **Parents, children and grandparents often all lived in the same house.** This family lived by the sea (which you can just see through the doorway). The painting is called *Good News From Abroad*; the letter was from someone in the family who was a sailor.

Having children was seen as the main reason for getting married. Often, there was only a year or two in age between each child in the family.

This photograph shows the family of a professional man – a doctor or a lawyer. It was taken in 1865. No matter how old they were, children living at home were expected to obey their fathers.

Men and women seldom lived together without being married, and most families had children. In rich families children were brought up by servants, and did not have much to do with their parents. Children of poor families spent more time with their parents, but from an early age they were expected to work and add to the family income.

Many families had relatives living with them. These were often older relations. Sometimes, though, brothers or sisters of the head of the house could be given a home if they fell on hard times. Children whose parents had died were usually taken in and brought up by close relatives.

Servants were an important part of life in all but the poorest families. They made family life possible, but were rarely treated as part of the family in the way that Prince Albert believed. In less well-off homes, servants did become part of the family and often were treated as equals.

HUSBANDS AND FATHERS

"What greater happiness can a man know than to sit at his own fireside of an evening, surrounded by his family?", said Prince Albert, the queen's husband. He enjoyed family life, so it became fashionable, especially in middle-class families, to follow his example. So what was a man's place in the family?

▽ **Shopkeepers' wives only served in the shop if they had to.** They were often far too busy caring for the younger children and looking after the home.

Good husbands and fathers were expected to provide their families with a home and money for food and clothes. But not all of them did this or could do so. Poor husbands and fathers worked if they could find a job. Some of them worked from home, weaving or making chairs or wooden toys. Often the whole family spent the day working together. They ate together, too.

▷ **A shopkeeper's family lived in rooms behind and above the shop.** The father expected his children to help in the shop as soon as they were old enough. Boys often learned their father's trade. The eldest son would inherit the family business when the father died.

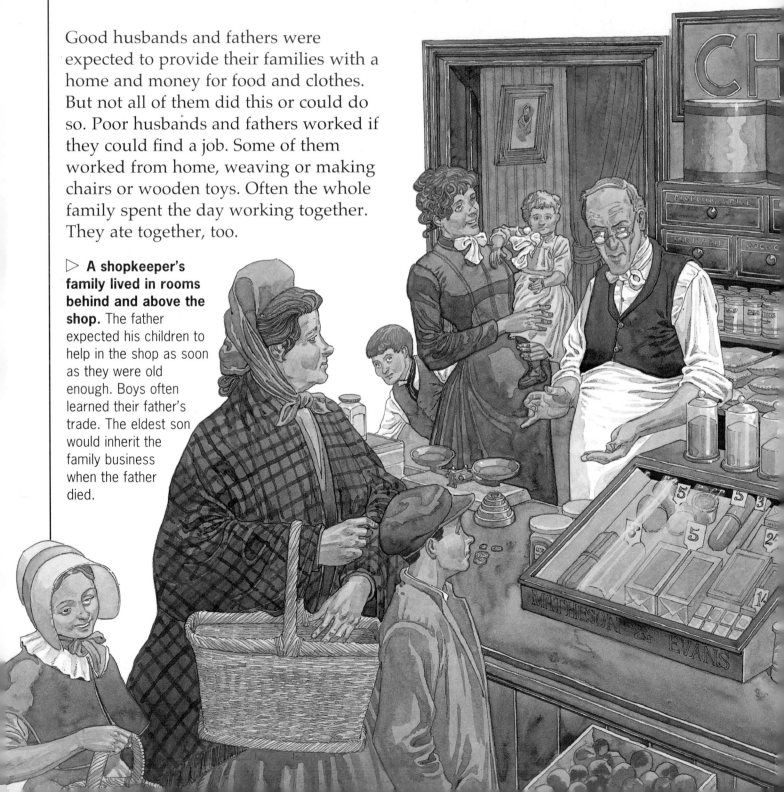

◁ **This painting captures the middle-class Victorian idea of a father at the heart of family life.** The father obviously looks after his family well. He has brought home a large Christmas hamper stuffed with good things. The slippers in the corner suggest he will stay at home in the evening, not go out by himself.

◁ **Food was not sold already weighed and packed,** as it is today. Here, the shopkeeper's eldest son is about to take down a large tin of tea and weigh out what the customer wants.

▷ **A Victorian advertisement for mustard.** Shopkeepers sold dry goods, such as mustard, flour, sugar and tea, from huge storage tins. Cheese was cut from big slabs.

Not every husband spent a lot of time at home. Wealthy men tended to spend most of their time with other wealthy men. In the country they went hunting or fishing. In the town they went out all day, maybe to a private club, where they smoked, drank, read the newspaper and ate lunch. They came home for dinner, especially if there was a party to give or go to.

Middle-class husbands often worked all day, in shops or offices. Many of them spent their evening playing games with their families. Others spent time in their study rooms on their own. Men with jobs in mines and factories spent long hours at work. In the evenings they often went out to avoid their cramped home. They might go to the nearest pub with friends, or to the Reading Rooms where, for a penny a week, working men could go to read each evening.

WIVES AND MOTHERS

**"Man for the field and woman for the hearth;
Man for the sword, and for the needle she;
Man with the head and woman with the heart;
Man to command and woman to obey." These lines
from a poem by Alfred, Lord Tennyson sum up how
Victorian men saw the role of women.**

Women were expected to marry. Most did, between the ages
of 18 and 22. (Most men married between the ages of 20 and
25.) Those who did not marry had restricted lives. Women
from a working-class family could go out to work. Some
unmarried women stayed at home, caring for their parents as
they got older. Such a life could be very dull. One young
woman, Florence Nightingale, who later left home and became
a famous nurse, wrote: "The evenings never seemed to end –
for how many years have I watched that drawing room clock
and thought it would never reach ten!"

▷ **A mother
organizes a family
birthday celebration**
in a middle-class home.
It was not until Victorian
times that people began
to celebrate birthdays in
a big way.

Here the family
gather round to watch
the presents being
unwrapped. The maid
is bringing in another
parcel. This
young boy is
lucky since he
has a lot of
presents –
most children
would get
only one.

▷ **Mrs Gertrude
Hutchinson and her
eldest son, Gordon.**
This photograph was
taken in about 1890,
soon after Gordon
had been christened.
Gordon died of a lung
disease when he was
just two years old.

In Victorian times,
babies – both boys and
girls – wore dresses
for the first year or two
of their lives. Often the
dresses were made for
them by their mothers.
Gordon Hutchinson is
probably wearing his
christening gown.
The patterns and sewing
on it would have been
done by hand, not
by machine.

Some women could not afford to stay at home. A visitor to a cotton spinning mill in 1839 reported: "The place was full of young women, some pregnant, all obliged to work, standing, for 12 hours a day. They were all very pale and thin." Women from poor families had to go out to work, even if their husbands worked. They also had to shop, clean and cook.

Rich and well-off women were often bored, with too little to do. All women were seen as inferior to men. When they married, everything they owned became their husband's property. If they worked, they were paid less for doing the same job as men. But by 1903, women were allowed to own property, and more of them were working for fair wages.

△ **The whole family help** a mother to work from home.

9

Babies and Young Children

"When little Fred went to bed, he always said his prayers. He kissed Mama and then Papa, and straightaway went upstairs." This Victorian nursery poem beautifully describes the ideal, well-behaved, obedient Victorian toddler.

▷ *A Street Fight* – a **Victorian painting.** Poor families were often large but their homes were small. So most of the children, even little ones, spent a lot of time outside, playing in the street or in the fields. Children played with all the other local children. In the country, these would be all the children from the village. In town, they would be the children from nearby streets. Older girls usually looked after the smallest children.

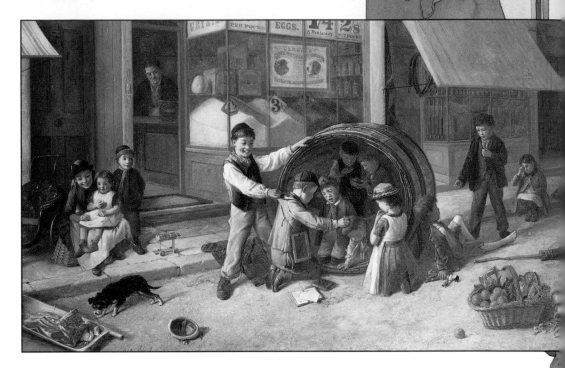

Not all Victorian babies and youngsters had lives that were as well organized as little Fred's. Many babies born into poor families died before their first birthday.

In Victorian times, most women gave birth to their babies at home. How safe this was depended on how rich they were. Rich people could hire a midwife and nurses to look after the mother and baby. They could also pay for regular visits from the local doctor. Poor families relied on neighbours for help. Their babies were born in homes that were cold, dirty and damp. Babies born into rich and middle-class families were much more likely to survive.

Upper-class children grew up in the nursery and schoolroom. They had lots of toys, but seldom played with other children. Middle-class boys and girls played with other children, but their friends were often chosen by the parents, not the children themselves. They had a few carefully chosen toys.

Poor children were often brought up by older sisters. Their toys and their clothes were often handed down from older brothers and sisters. They spent a lot of time outside the home, playing in large groups. If a family had too many children, the baby might be sent to live with relatives.

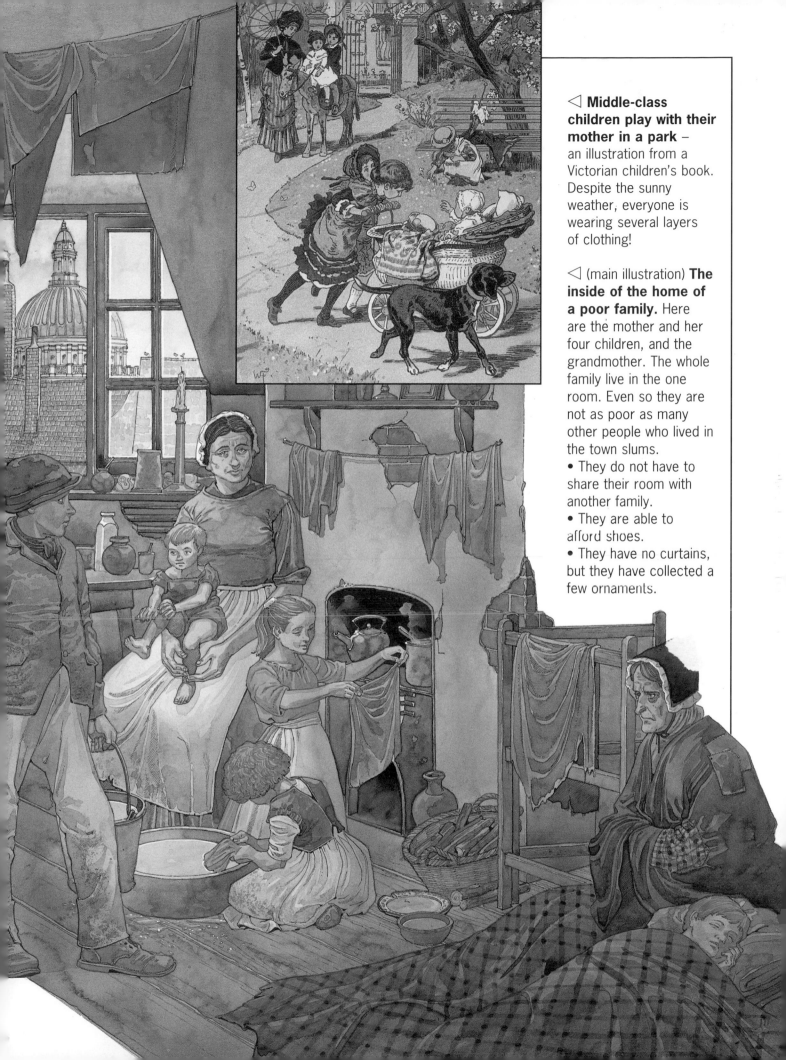

◁ **Middle-class children play with their mother in a park** – an illustration from a Victorian children's book. Despite the sunny weather, everyone is wearing several layers of clothing!

◁ (main illustration) **The inside of the home of a poor family.** Here are the mother and her four children, and the grandmother. The whole family live in the one room. Even so they are not as poor as many other people who lived in the town slums.

• They do not have to share their room with another family.

• They are able to afford shoes.

• They have no curtains, but they have collected a few ornaments.

OLDER CHILDREN

"When I was little, I minded sheep and ran errands. In 1890, when I was about ten, I went down the pit [coal mine]. It was hard work, but we all did it, even kids who stayed at school until they were fourteen," a man who grew up in Yorkshire remembers.

Many Victorian children began work at an early age. All children were expected to learn to behave as adults and learn adult manners as soon as they could.

Upper-class girls went with their mothers to visit other families and sat drinking tea and talking politely. Some of them went to 'finishing schools' abroad, where they learned 'social skills', such as how to deal with servants!

Poor girls were expected to look after the younger children and help around the house. It was considered good training for married life.

▷ **In the living-room.** Older girls in less well-off families spent a lot of time looking after younger children. It was not just hard work. Some jobs, like bathing the baby, could become a game everyone enjoyed.

▽ **Children dancing round a lamp-post.** Children had to make up their own games. There were no television, radio or computer games.

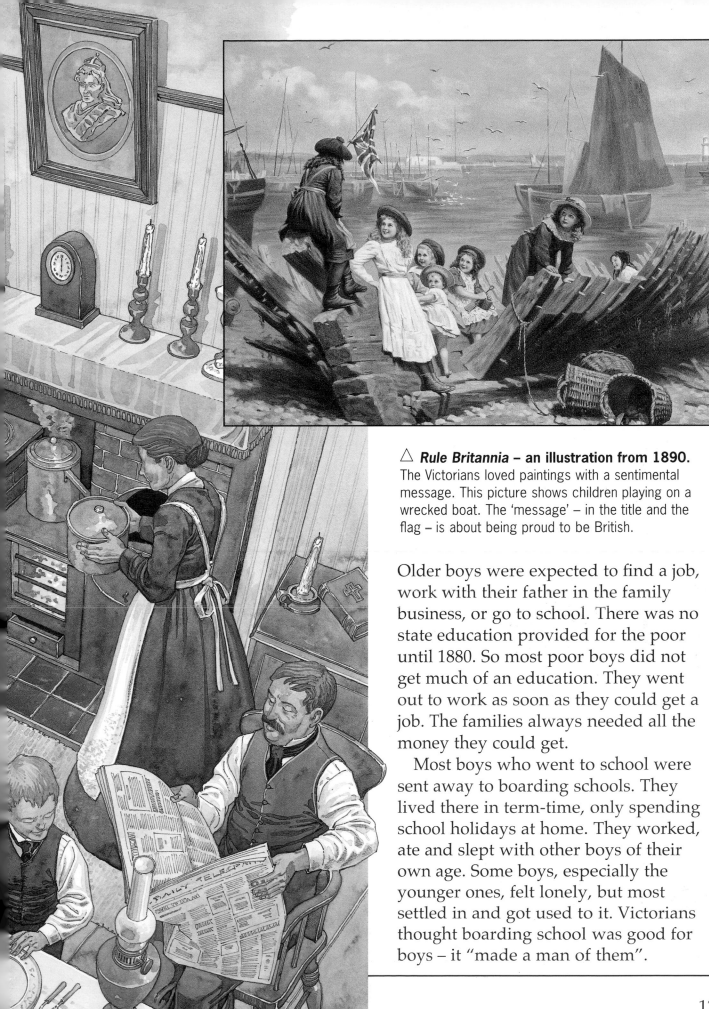

△ *Rule Britannia* – **an illustration from 1890.**
The Victorians loved paintings with a sentimental
message. This picture shows children playing on a
wrecked boat. The 'message' – in the title and the
flag – is about being proud to be British.

Older boys were expected to find a job,
work with their father in the family
business, or go to school. There was no
state education provided for the poor
until 1880. So most poor boys did not
get much of an education. They went
out to work as soon as they could get a
job. The families always needed all the
money they could get.

Most boys who went to school were
sent away to boarding schools. They
lived there in term-time, only spending
school holidays at home. They worked,
ate and slept with other boys of their
own age. Some boys, especially the
younger ones, felt lonely, but most
settled in and got used to it. Victorians
thought boarding school was good for
boys – it "made a man of them".

RELATIVES

"You ought not to think yourself equal to your cousins because their mother kindly allows you to be brought up with them. They will have a great deal of money: you will have none. It is your place to be humble," a maid says in the book *Jane Eyre*. She sums up clearly the position in Victorian times of people forced to depend on the kindness of relatives.

People who were struck by disaster, or those who were just too old to work, could turn to relatives for help, or they could go to the workhouse. These people included families with no work and nowhere to live, and old people who had not been able to save any money during their working lives.

If both parents in a family died, leaving their children orphans, those children had to be brought up by someone else. If the children inherited money, it could be used to make sure they were brought up in some sort of comfort. But orphans were usually taken in by relations or sent to the workhouse. Some children were lucky. They were taken in by relatives who cared about them. They were made part of the family. Others, like Jane Eyre in the book by Charlotte Bronte, were very badly treated and constantly reminded that they should be grateful for any kindness shown to them.

▷ **Most families tried to look after their elderly relatives.** Often the grandmother would look after the children while the mother worked in the house, as here, or at a nearby factory, mill or farm.

▷ **A family visits its sick grandmother in the women's ward of a workhouse.** The grandfather, too, lives in the workhouse, but he has not seen his wife for days. The family can no longer afford for the grandparents to live with them.

Victorian governments did not pay pensions or unemployment benefit. If poor and homeless people could not get help from the church or relatives, they had to go to workhouses.

▷ **Dinner time in the men's side at Marylebone Workhouse in London –** a photograph taken in about 1900. Food for the workers would have been mostly porridge or soup, bread and weak tea.

The people who ran workhouses did not want to encourage people to come there. They made them uncomfortable, and had separate buildings for men and women, which split up families.

SERVANTS

"Servants should obey their masters and please them well in all things," said a text that was painted on the walls of the kitchen of many large houses. Servants may have been part of the family, but they were expected to know their place and keep to it.

▷ **Rich people often had their servants photographed,** as here and in the illustration below. The photo, taken in 1870, is of servants from a wealthy home.

△ **The head gardener** holds the latest type of lawn mower. The boy on his left helps him in the greenhouses.

△ **One of the three maids** holds a duster for cleaning the house. The housekeeper, the main servant, sits by them.

◁ **This Victorian painting shows a few of the servants of a grand house having afternoon tea.** Servants did get some time off work. Also, there was less for them to do in the middle of the afternoon. Their visitor is an ex-servant who has left to get married. The footman is making so much noise that no one has heard the cook – seen through the door – returning.

The 1891 census (a count of the country's population) showed that there were more servants than any other sort of worker. There were 1,386,167 women and 58,527 men 'in service'. These figures included women who worked as housekeepers for men who had no wife to run the home. One in every twelve of these servants was under the age of 15. Most servants lived in the family house. But some, especially those who worked in smaller houses, had their own homes and came to work each day.

Rich people needed lots of servants to run their homes, and these servants became part of an invisible army – part of the 'family' and necessary to it, but hardly noticed at all. They each had clearly defined jobs to do in the home.

Not all servants worked in big houses. Many servants, especially women, were the only servant in a relatively poor household. They cooked, cleaned, washed and sewed, depending on what needed doing. In many cases they also ran errands, did the shopping and looked after the children. This could mean that they became part of the family. But some of them were treated extremely badly by their employers, and could feel very lonely. By contrast, in a big house there was usually someone to tell their troubles to.

△ **The cook** sits on the bench with a pot, next to the nanny, while the boot–boy holds a brush for polishing boots.

△ **The coachman** holds a whip for driving the family coach. The stable-boy is ready to clean out the stables.

THE HOME

"I have comfortable enough lodgings," a customs officer wrote home in 1836, **"but yet it is Home Sweet Home I long for".** The home was at the heart of Victorian family life. Everyone had a part to play in family life. They also had, more often than not, a particular place in the home.

Wealthy people had large houses and made clear rules about who went where. The servants slept in the attics and worked in the basement. They had their own set of 'back stairs' connecting the two, so they could come and go without using the stairs in the main part of the house. Children stayed in the nurseries and schoolroom, unless invited into the adult part of the house. The library, billiard room and gun room were used mainly by the men, leaving the drawing rooms to the ladies.

Most middle-class people had smaller houses with fewer rooms. The servants still had the attics and the basement, but did not have a separate stairway. The head of the house had a study, while all the children had just one room, called the nursery or schoolroom depending on the children's ages. These houses needed fewer servants to run them. Middle-class people did not entertain like the upper-classes, who invited dozens of people to stay and so needed lots of bedrooms.

Less well-off people often rented out a room in their house to a lodger, who paid them weekly for it. Sometimes they just rented out the room, but often they cooked and washed for the lodger too, charging him or her more money if they did so.

Poor families lived in just one room. They did not have servants. The room had separate places for cooking, eating and sleeping. The poorest families shared a room with other families. For privacy, they tried to divide up the room with curtains.

△ **Poor people's cottages could be very bare.** But even this was better than no home at all. These Irish people have been thrown out of their home for not paying their rent. Their things are piled up in the rain.

▷ **The Doctor, painted in 1868.** Children in small homes played outside or in the living-room, like these children. Everyone is pretending to mix medicines or to be a nurse. Perhaps they have seen their mother do these for their grandmother.

◁ **These children are playing in their nursery.** They have a big dolls' house to play with. The girls are putting all the toy people into the right rooms in the house.
• The cook is in the kitchen, getting the dinner.
• The lady of the house is in the living-room.
Victorian playthings encouraged children to behave as adults.

19

FAMILY OUTINGS

"A few years ago a visit to the seaside was a luxury well beyond the means of any worker," remarked the travel agent, Thomas Cook, in the 1850s. Cook arranged holidays 'for all pockets'. His cheap trips were made possible by using rail travel.

▷ **At the seaside.** Outside, most people wore hats and ladies frequently carried sunshades (below right). It was not fashionable to have a suntan.

▷ **Hyde Park, London, painted by John Ritchie in 1858.** All sorts of people went to the park, some for the day, others just for an hour or so. There was no charge to go into the park. There were places to sit and lots of things to see and do. Look for:
• rich people being driven in their carriage.
• two toddlers in pushchairs.
• some poor children coming to the pond.
• an elderly couple taking a rest from walking the dog.
• a soldier in uniform.
• a man fishing.
• a boy with a toy boat.

Families have always gone on outings for special treats. In Victorian times, they went to the circus, the funfair or the zoo. But it was not until the 1890s that family holidays became something that many people went on.

Rail travel meant people could go further, faster and more cheaply than before. There was an explosion of cheap excursions, with rail travel and cheap lodgings included in the price. These were often run on 'special' trains, which were crammed full of 'day trippers'.

Thomas Cook also arranged trips to other places. He laid on trips to the Great Exhibition in London in 1851. He arranged tours of cathedral cities and 'educational' trips, not for children, but for working people who wanted to learn things. But most of his customers wanted to go to the seaside, if only for the day. The well-to-do found seaside resorts that had been 'select' were now horrifyingly 'low'. Some towns discouraged excursions, in the hope of keeping their regular, wealthy visitors.

So where could well-off families go to escape? Thomas Cook had the answer. Professional families crossed the Channel by boat to French beaches. Italy and Switzerland, reached by boat and rail, were popular destinations. Even on holidays, the rich kept themselves apart from middle-class and working-class people. They stayed at hotels that only rich people could afford.

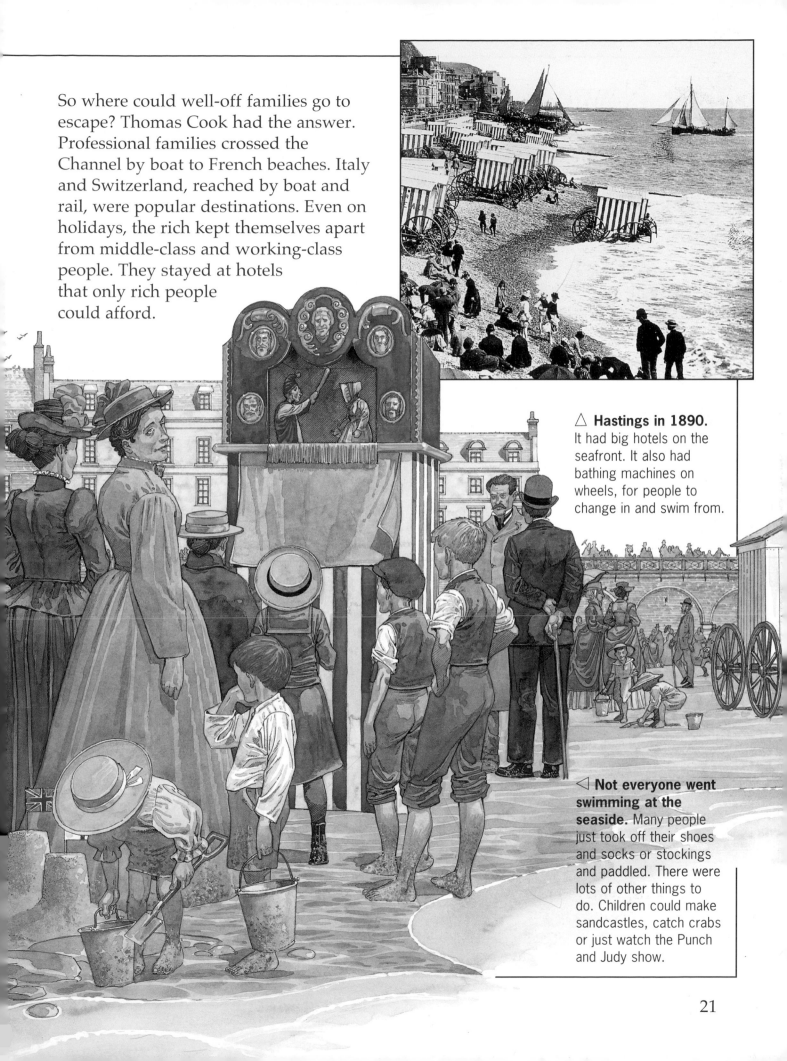

△ **Hastings in 1890.** It had big hotels on the seafront. It also had bathing machines on wheels, for people to change in and swim from.

◁ **Not everyone went swimming at the seaside.** Many people just took off their shoes and socks or stockings and paddled. There were lots of other things to do. Children could make sandcastles, catch crabs or just watch the Punch and Judy show.

21

NOW AND THEN

"I'd have hated being in a Victorian family," said a schoolboy in 1997. "You had to do what you were told all the time, and there were germs and no radio or computers." Is family life different now?

Nowadays, families are smaller – most people have just one or two children, and fewer families have relatives living with them. There are special homes for the old and orphans, and fewer homeless people. Family homes, too, are smaller.

While rich people still live in homes that are luxurious, they are not as big and difficult to run. This is partly because it is harder now to find enough people to do the work to run huge houses. There are less people willing to do the work of servants than there used to be. But there are a lot of machines, such as dishwashers and washing machines, that help people do the housework more quickly.

Today, many families can afford to go on holiday more than once a year, and often visit other countries.

▽ *Charity* – **by Victorian artist Thomas Brooks.** Without a national health service, Victorian families had to pay for their medical treatment. Poor people could not afford to call the doctor. Better-off women, like the one in this painting, went to visit the local sick people, taking food and sometimes medicine that a poor family could not afford to buy.

◁ **Victorian families were bigger than families now.** In wealthy and middle-class homes they were looked after by a 'nanny', or nanny and 'nurserymaid' – a young girl training as a nanny. In this photo, taken in 1880, there are two nannies (sitting) and two nurserymaids. The child sitting on the floor is a boy.

Glossary

attic a room just under the roof of a building.

boarding schools schools where children 'board' – live there in term-time – for which the parents pay fees.

boot-boy the boy in a big house whose job is to clean the boots and shoes of the family, guests and servants.

carriage a horse-drawn vehicle, often driven by a coachman (servant).

census a count of the population made every 10 years by the government. As well as names and ages of people, the census asks details of jobs, too.

coachman a servant who drives his employer's horse-drawn carriage.

cotton-spinning mill a factory where lots of machines are used to spin fibres from cotton plants into thread.

croquet a game where you knock balls through a set of hoops.

excursions trips or outings.

finishing schools boarding schools where girls are 'finished' – prepared to be a good wife by being taught to dance, sing, embroider and speak a little French and maybe German and Spanish.

footman a servant in a big house who works in the main house, not the kitchens or garden. He takes messages, opens doors, and sometimes helps to serve dinner.

hearth the stone or tile part of the floor in front of a fireplace.

household everyone living in the same house.

inferior less important.

inherited something received from a person on their death.

lodgings a place to stay (usually a room in someone else's home) when away from home.

middle class people who, in Victorian times, were seen as neither rich and important nor poor and unimportant. Doctors, shopkeepers and lawyers were middle class.

midwives nurses who look after women while they are pregnant, while they are having the baby, and while the baby is very young.

ornaments decorative things like vases and china models of people and animals.

orphan a child whose parents are both dead.

park an area of land, usually with trees, often with animals grazing in it, that is near the big house of an estate.

professionals people who have a job that needs special training and a certain level of education. Lawyers, doctors and teachers are all professional people.

slums parts of towns where poor people live crammed into badly built and uncared for houses.

stable-boy boy who looks after horses on a farm or country estate.

upper class people who were seen in Victorian times as rich and important. Upper class people did not have to work every day to make a living.

well-off people who had a lot of money, but were not as rich as others.

workhouse a place that gave homeless people somewhere to sleep and some food in return for work.

working class people who were seen as poor and unimportant in Victorian times. They had to work all the time for a living, usually working for other people. Miners, shop workers, factory workers and servants were working class.

1837 Victoria became Queen of England.

1842 Law passed to stop women and children below the age of 10 working underground in mines.

1847 Law passed to stop women and children below the age of 18 working over 10 hours a day in factories.

1845-50s Famine in Ireland and Scotland, and disease in major cities in England, killed thousands of people each week.

1851 Great Exhibition held in London. Families came from all over the world to look at the things on show there.

1854 Crimean War started. Many fathers went away to fight.

1867 Law made to stop children below the age of 8 working in any factory or workshop.

1881 Married Women's Property Act passed to allow women to own their own property, rather than give it to their husband when they married.

1901 Victoria died. Her eldest son became King Edward VII.

INDEX

Victorian Family Life

Jane Shuter

Illustrated by John James

Heinemann

HISTORY OF BRITAIN – VICTORIAN FAMILY LIFE
was produced for Heinemann Children's Reference
by Lionheart Books, London.

Editor: Lionel Bender
Designer: Ben White
Editorial Assistant: Madeleine Samuel
Picture Researcher: Jennie Karrach
Media Conversion and Typesetting: Michael Weintroub, Lionel Bender
Editorial Advisors: Andrew Farrow, Paul Shuter

Production Controller: Lorraine Stebbing
Editorial Director: David Riley

First published in Great Britain in 1997 by
Heinemann Educational Publishers, a division of
Reed Educational and Professional Publishing Limited,
Halley Court, Jordan Hill, Oxford OX2 8EJ.

MADRID ATHENS
FLORENCE PRAGUE WARSAW
PORTSMOUTH NH CHICAGO SAO PAULO MEXICO
SINGAPORE TOKYO MELBOURNE AUCKLAND
IBADAN GABORONE JOHANNESBURG KAMPALA NAIROBI

© Reed Educational & Professional Publishing Ltd 1997

Heinemann is a registered trademark of Reed Educational & Professional
Publishing Limited.

ISBN 0431 05721 4 Hb   ISBN 0431 05734 6 Pb

British Library Cataloguing-in-Publication Data.
A catalogue record for this book is available
from the British Library.

Printed in Italy

Acknowledgements
Picture credits
Page 4: Fine Art Photographic Library Ltd./Courtesy of Fine Art of
Oakham. 5: The Hulton Getty Picture Collection Limited. 7 (top): Fine Art
Photographic Library Ltd. 7 (centre right): Mary Evans Picture Library.
8: The Hulton Getty Picture Collection Limited. 9: Fine Art Photographic
Library Ltd./Courtesy of Haynes Fine Art, Broadway. 10: Fine Art
Photographic Library Ltd. 11: Mary Evans Picture Library. 12: The Hulton
Deutsch Collection Limited. 13, 14: Mary Evans Picture Library. 15: Fine
Art Photographic Library Ltd. 16: The Hulton Deutsch Collection Limited.
17: Fine Art Photographic Library Ltd. 18: Mary Evans Picture Library.
19: Fine Art Photographic Library Ltd. 20: The Museum of London.
21: The Hulton Deutsch Collection Limited. 22 (left): The Hulton Deutsch
Collection Limited. 22 (right): Fine Art Photographic Library Ltd.

Artwork credits
All artwork by John James

Cover: Artwork by John James; photo Hulton Deutsch Collection Limited.

PLACES TO VISIT

Angus Folk Museum, Glamis, Scotland.
A reconstructed street of houses, showing working-class village family life.

Brantwood, Coniston, Lake District. Home and lands of John Ruskin, a Victorian artist and writer.

Cecil Higgins Art Gallery and Museum, Bedford.
A furnished Victorian grand house.

Fasque, Fettercairn, Grampian, Scotland. A large Victorian country house, furnished to give a lived-in feel.

Gunnersbury Park Museum, Gunnersbury Park, London. Victorian rooms and themed exhibitions that change regularly. Has a costume collection.

Highland Folk Museum, Kingussie, Scotland. Recreated family homes; country family life is well displayed.

Hughenden Manor, near High Wycombe, Bucks. The home of Benjamin Disraeli, a British Prime Minister in Victorian times.

Linley Sambourne House, 18 Stafford Terrace, Kensington, London. A late-Victorian town house. Has furniture, decorations and everyday objects, a good example of a well-off family's home.

Osborne House, Isle of Wight. Queen Victoria's seaside home. Includes play houses for her children.

Peckover House and Garden, North Brink, Cambridgeshire. A good example of a Victorian house with gardens.

Preston Manor, Preston Park, Brighton, Sussex.
A Victorian family home away from the town. Has lots of everyday objects of the period.

Shugborough House, East Grinstead, West Sussex.
Being reconstructed as a working country estate.
Especially good examples of the work of servants on a large Victorian estate.

Sudbury Hall and National Trust Museum of Childhood, near Derby, Derbyshire. Good displays on children and the home.

The Tenement House, 145 Buccleuch Street, Glasgow. A late-Victorian home of a family less well-off than most.

Torosay Castle and Gardens, Isle of Mull. An early Victorian house and gardens.

Wallington House, Northumberland. Beautiful Victorian house and grounds.

Welsh Folk Museum, St. Fagin's, Cardiff. Recreated homes, farm, chapel and school mostly dating from late-Victorian times.